# A Bed for Red Hen

By Cameron Macintosh

Peg has hens in a run.

# The run is a big net.

# Peg met Red Hen.

I can get a bed
for Red Hen!

Peg gets the bed.

It is a **dog** bed!

Red Hen can see the bed.

But Red Hen sits in the mud!

Peg is sad.

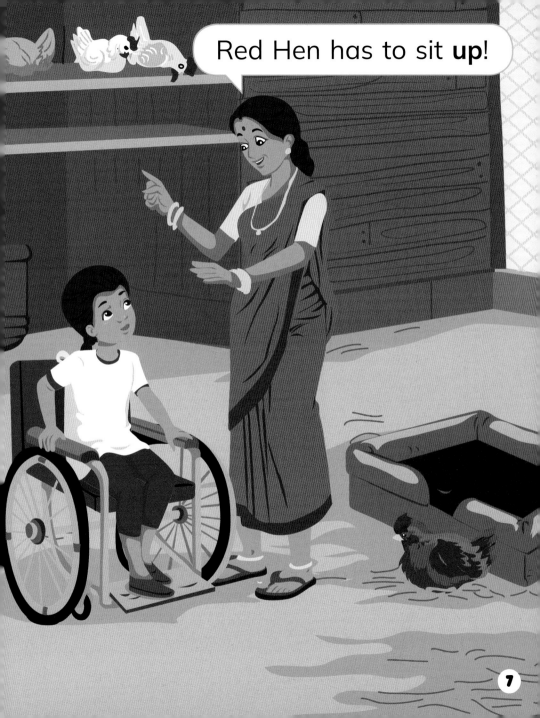

7

Peg and Mum get a big rod for Red Hen.

Red Hen sits on the rod.

Peg is not sad.

The rod is a bed for Red Hen!

# CHECKING FOR MEANING

1. Where are Peg's hens at the start of the story? *(Literal)*

2. What made Peg sad? *(Literal)*

3. Why does the run for the hens have a big net? *(Inferential)*

# EXTENDING VOCABULARY

| | |
|---|---|
| **Peg** | Make words that rhyme with *Peg* by taking away the *p* and putting other letters at the start of the word. What do these words mean? |
| **run** | Find the word *run*. What does this word mean in this story? What is a different meaning of the word *run*? |
| **rod** | How many sounds are there in the word *rod*? What are they? What does *rod* mean? Can you think of another word that has the same meaning? |

# MOVING BEYOND THE TEXT

1. Why do you think Peg wanted to get a bed for Red Hen?

2. Where do other animals sleep?

3. What do hens' feet look like? Why are they like this?

4. Where do hens sit when they lay eggs?

# SPEED SOUNDS

| | | | | |
|---|---|---|---|---|
| Dd | Jj | Oo | Gg | Uu |

| | | | | | |
|---|---|---|---|---|---|
| Cc | Bb | Rr | Ee | Ff | Hh | Nn |

| | | | | |
|---|---|---|---|---|
| Mm | Ss | Aa | Pp | Ii | Tt |

# PRACTICE WORDS

Peg

run

big

Red

get

bed

dog

mud

up

on

sad

rod

Mum

gets

not

and

But